ISBN 978-1-334-47074-5
PIBN 10739213

1 MONTH OF
FREE
READING

at
www.ForgottenBooks.com

By purchasing this book you are eligible for one month membership to ForgottenBooks.com, giving you unlimited access to our entire collection of over 700,000 titles via our web site and mobile apps.

To claim your free month visit:
www.forgottenbooks.com/free739213

America's Opportunity
in Foreign Investments

Guaranty Trust Company
of New York

GIFT

America's Opportunity in Foreign Investments

Guaranty Trust Company of New York

140 Broadway

FIFTH AVENUE OFFICE
Fifth Avenue and 43rd Street

MADISON AVENUE OFFICE
Madison Avenue and 60th Street

LONDON OFFICES
32 Lombard Street, E. C.
5 Lower Grosvenor Pl., S. W.

LIVERPOOL OFFICE
27 Cotton Exchange Buildings

PARIS OFFICE
1 & 3 Rue des Italiens

HAVRE OFFICE
122 Boulevard Strasbourg

BRUSSELS OFFICE
158 Rue Royale

America's Opportunity in Foreign Investments

THE World War has created an opportunity for America by hastening the time when America should play a more important part in world trade and world finance. It is imperative that the investing public should not overlook our present opportunities. The necessity of maintaining our position in world trade, of keeping markets open for our products, emphasizes the need for financing our export trade through extension of credit abroad and purchase of foreign securities.

The rapid development of the extensive new areas of the United States was made possible by the investment of capital from other countries. The continued investment of capital in combination with our nationalistic policy encouraged the development of a diversified industry which, during the period of our expansion, found the market for its products within the country. Our industries grew to such an extent that many producers became interested in foreign trade as an outlet for their products. The recent World War led to a further expansion of our industrial capacity and-the establishment of comparatively new industries. The maintenance of an outlet for our products in other countries is essential to the well-being of American industries. The investment of capital in other countries is one of the effective ways to keep world markets open for American products. This involves the purchase of foreign securities and the development of an international finance market in this country.

The World War changed this country from a borrowing to a lending nation and set in operation forces that will make this country an increasingly important lender of capital.

As we are entering this period of development it is well to consider what other countries have done, what methods they have used to obtain outlets for their surplus of capital. As their wealth increased and they were able to lend large amounts, Amsterdam, London, Paris, Brussels, and Berlin became in their turn financial centers, to which all countries, but especially those seeking to develop new sources of wealth, looked for assistance through credit extensions. When the fleets of the Netherlands dominated the seas and the possession of the rich islands in the Far East gave them predominance in world trade, Amsterdam was the financial center of the world. It lost its predominance to London after the Napoleonic Wars. Later, the industrial development on the continent of Europe led to the development of important financial centers at Paris, Brussels, and Berlin.

We must not rest with a passive recognition of the opportunities of America in foreign trade and in the foreign investment field. We individually must do our utmost to induce the public and our financial leaders to play the great part which has been made possible. It takes vision and courage to venture out into new activities which will lead to an expansion of world trade. The American public should understand the necessity of investing in foreign securities and the relation that it bears to our own industrial and economic life.

Growth of Great Britain as a Creditor Nation

For a long time before the war the pre-eminence of London as a financial center was everywhere recognized. The great trading routes went through English ports. In all the principal markets of the world payments for goods were made by means of drafts on London drawn in pounds sterling and traders considered them as good as gold because of the existence in London of a wide market where they could be disposed of for cash. Through world-wide trade connections the English financiers had developed an international point of view, so that men from every country going to London to seek capital for new enterprises felt sure that their plans would get a sympathetic hearing and that in all probability the money or credit required would be forthcoming.

This position in finance and trade to which London attained is indicated by the variety of the securities which are listed on the London Stock Exchange. The character and number of foreign and colonial securities listed is as follows:

Colonial and Provincial Government Securities	185
Indian and Colonial City Securities	176
Foreign Cities	76
Foreign Government Securities	210
Railways in British Colonial Possessions	110
Indian Railways	68
American Railroad Securities	56
Foreign Railways	276
Total	1,157

The total number of domestic securities of the United Kingdom in these same classes is as follows:

British Funds	72
City and County	176
Public Bonds	34
Railways, Shares, Stocks & Debentures	361
Total	643

In addition to these there are many commercial and industrial securities which cannot be readily classified, it being uncertain to what extent they are domestic and to what extent they are foreign, because of the overlapping of the interests which they represent. But the number of foreign and colonial securities is certainly greater than the number of domestic securities.

Investment in foreign enterprises had begun in a small way in the sixteenth and seventeenth centuries. The industrial revolution in the middle of the eighteenth century created a great demand for capital with which to obtain machinery, to build new factories, and to develop coal mines. The prolonged wars of this period forced the Government to borrow heavily from the English people and also from other countries. Money rates were high and Dutch capitalists took advantage of the situation to invest very large amounts in the bonds and notes issued by the British Government, in stock of the Bank of England, and in commercial or industrial enterprises. Amsterdam at that time was the chief financial center of the world. At the end of the century Great Britain was still a borrowing nation.

During the Napoleonic Wars little progress was made by Englishmen in extending their foreign enterprises. All the capital and credit available were needed at home to finance the war, to provide subsidies amounting to $219,-859,000 for the country's Allies, and to keep up the development of industrial

[4]

enterprises. This imposed great burdens on the people for a time. Everything in the land was taxed to the limit of endurance, but at the end of the war the industrial capacity of England had been expanded, a sizeable merchant marine had been built, and the people had learned how to save money. There began immediately a rapid development of British foreign investment. Carried forward by the same spirit which had enabled them to overcome Napoleon, the people of the British Isles took the utmost advantage of their expanded productive capacity and of their experience in saving and investing. Important loans were made to the continental countries which had suffered the most from the long years of war and foreign holdings of British bonds and stocks were bought back from the Dutch and others.

With this effort to get out of debt and to buy into foreign enterprises there went an increase in trading with foreign countries everywhere. This expansion of world trade, which became pronounced about 1820, led to important investments in South American mines, and loans to the South American Governments. American canal and railway bonds, as well as bonds issued by various State Governments, were readily taken by English investors. French and Belgian railroad securities also found a market in London. The disturbances in Europe and the growth of France and other continental countries led British investors in the latter part of the first half of the century to seek more profitable openings in America. After our Civil War investors turned their attention to the British Colonies, to South America, South Africa, and the Far East.

Distribution of British   The foreign
Foreign Investments   investments
               of Great
Britain, as estimated by Sir George Paish

in 1913, were mainly in railways and government securities, as indicated by the following table, in which the value of the pound sterling is taken as $4.8665.

Railways	$7,402,014,631.50
Government Securities	4,669,518,679.50
Mines	1,327,527,668.50
Finance Land & Invest	1,188,336,035.50
Municipal	718,037,475.00
Commerce and Industrial	707,258,178.00
Tramways	378,565,035.00
Banks	354,811,648.50

While there was a wide distribution of British investments throughout the world, the largest amounts were invested in the colonial possessions, in the United States and in the Argentine Republic, as shown by the following:

INDIA AND COLONIES

Canada and Newfoundland	$2,505,614,855.00
Australia	1,616,223,048.00
New Zealand	410,411,411.00
South Africa	1,801,539,368.00
West Africa	181,544,782.50
India and Ceylon	1,843,313,404.00
Straits Settlements	132,821,384.50
Hongkong	15,105,616.00
British North Borneo	28,323,030.00
Other Colonies	127,448,768.50
Total India and Colonies	$8,662,345,667.50

FOREIGN COUNTRIES

United States	$3,672,343,630.50
Cuba	160,959,487.50
Philippines	39,988,030.50
Argentina	1,555,163,072.50
Brazil	718,125,072.50
Mexico	481,875,963.50
Chile	297,552,409.50
Uruguay	175,797,446.00
Peru	166,302,904.50
Miscellaneous American	124,280,677.00
Russia	324,240,295.50
Egypt	218,564,248.00
Spain	92,740,890.50
Turkey	90,984,084.00
Italy	60,539,260.00
Portugal	39,593,844.00
France	39,029,330.00
Germany	30,970,406.00

[5]

Miscellaneous European	265,613,570.00
Japan	305,694,064.00
China	213,556,619.50
Miscellaneous Foreign	339,180,450.50
Total Foreign	$ 9,413,095,756.00
Grand Total	$18,075,441,423.50

This total does not include a large amount of capital privately invested abroad and, were this added, the total British investments in the colonies and in foreign countries would amount, as estimated, to $19,466,000,000.

Bases for
Wide Distribution
The wide distribution of securities on the London Stock Exchange has been an outgrowth of Great Britain's extensive trade relations, of British colonial expansion, of the settlement of English-speaking people in many countries, and of the establishment there of institutions similar to those of England. Through the participation of the British mercantile marine in trade with all countries, England became the clearing house and transshipping center for world trade. Out of this trade the imposing structure of British overseas investments developed. Wherever ships went, capital followed and was invested freely in the enterprises of every nation, thus insuring the continuance of trade and its increase as these enterprises enlarged their activities.

British investors, compared with investors in other countries, have generally acted as pioneers in discovering and opening up new areas for development. After the enterprise became stabilized it was possible to transfer a part of the capital to other countries, and thus British capital advanced continually into the more distant and less developed parts of the world. These new countries produced raw materials which industrial England needed. Like all new countries, they paid high rates of return on capital invested in their enterprises. They offered opportunities gradually to increase England's control of their trade and industry.

Influence of Foreign Investments upon Great Britain
The investment of capital in other countries, the extensive trade relations of Great Britain with other countries, the reliance upon other markets for the growing output of British industry, and the dependence upon many countries for sources of raw materials, have been bound up very closely with British economic life. The influence of British institutions in civilized countries and the wide-spread settlement of English-speaking people have been in part the outgrowth of Great Britain's policy of economic expansion. It is impossible to picture the conditions of living, the economic life of the British Isles, if business had only been national in scope and there had been no effort to expand their interests beyond their own boundaries.

Foreign Capital
in the United States
Ever since its discovery America has attracted the investment of European capital. It was because of the opportunities which they saw to develop trade—a market for their own wares and a source of raw materials for their home industries —that merchants of England, France, Spain, and Holland formed companies to promote colonizations in this Hemisphere. Their willingness to invest made possible the obtaining of ships to bring the colonists here and of supplies to sustain them until they had established themselves.

As the colonies grew in strength and importance more capital was imported for the development of tobacco and cotton plantations, and for mercantile

[6]

purposes. The large merchants were the investing class. The population of the American colonies was swelled by emigration from the United Kingdom, which naturally brought with it considerable supplies of capital. Attracted by the opportunities for trade and industry, enterprising men came to America from all parts of Europe. The War of Independence for a time checked the investment of British capital here, and as a result, considerable Dutch capital entered the country.

In 1800 no American securities were quoted in what was then regarded as the official list of the London Stock Exchange, but in 1825 nine issues of United States Government bonds and a number of state and city bonds were quoted in London. In 1820 there began a period of extensive canal and highway construction. The most important of these undertakings was the Erie Canal, which in 1825 connected the Atlantic Coast with the great agricultural regions west of the Allegheny Mountains. This was a period of extensive investment of foreign capital in America. From 1830 to 1840 the imports exceeded the exports by about $200,000,000, which may be taken as an indication of the amount of foreign capital invested here. In 1839 President Jackson estimated that the total accumulated investments of European capital was about $200,000,000.

A period of active railroad building in the forties and fifties brought into this country additional sums of foreign capital. The first American railway loan floated in London was that brought out by Baring Brothers in 1846, an issue of $2,000,000 of Baltimore & Ohio Railroad bonds. Considerable Dutch capital was invested in American securities during this period. The outbreak of the Civil War led many Europeans to dispose of their American securities. Because of their interest in the production of cotton in the Southern States, British and Dutch capitalists were reluctant to invest in Federal Government bonds. On the other hand, the investors of Germany took an active interest in United States bonds because there had been a large Teutonic immigration to this country in the forties and fifties. In 1866 the total amount of French and British capital in this country was estimated at only $350,000,000, but by 1869 it had increased to $1,000,000,000.

The total amount of all foreign capital invested in the United States was estimated by Mr. Wells in 1869 to be $1,465,-000,000. The greatest share belonged to British investors, but substantial amounts were held by Holland and Germany. In the early seventies extensive railway construction made possible still larger investments of foreign capital in this country. It is estimated that these increased from $243,000,000 in 1869 to $345,000,000 in 1876.

In the eighties and nineties foreign capital became interested in a variety of enterprises other than railways, particularly in mining, agriculture, manufacturing plants, and public utilities. The development of industrial combinations and the formation of large corporations, made attractive conditions for foreign capital seeking to enter the general industrial field.

In a report made to the United States Monetary Commission in 1910 Sir George Paish estimated that the total amount of foreign capital, including bank loans, invested in the United States was approximately six and one half billion dollars. Domestic capital, meanwhile, had been accumulating and while we continued to borrow, our capitalists were able, on the other hand, to make advances for the development of neighboring countries, especially Canada, Cuba, Mexico, and some of the South American countries. At the time Paish estimated that the total investment of American capital in foreign countries amounted to about one and one-half billion dollars, leaving America a debtor nation to the extent of about five billion dollars.

The capital which America obtained from abroad was used chiefly in extending and improving the railroads of the country. No one can survey the remarkable growth in the population, wealth, and productiveness of the United States without being impressed by the great part which the railroads have played. They made possible the cultivation of vast tracts of agricultural land, the produce of which before the war was valued at more than eight billion dollars. They made possible the opening up of our immense stores of minerals. In other directions the investment of foreign capital here was invaluable. It enabled the American people to devote their own savings to the building and furnishing of homes, to the equipment of their manufactories, and to fitting out retail establishments; and in this way accelerated the growth of population and wealth.

Sir George Paish estimates that the increase in the annual production of wealth in the United States made possible by the investment of foreign capital here has been at least twenty times greater than the sum paid for interest. The interest paid to foreign capitalists by the United States has been of less importance to those capitalists than the increase in the wealth of this country which their investments made possible. Such increase in our wealth has meant increased buying power, and demand for the products of the lending country so that the returns from the foreign investment have been indefinitely larger than the mere interest payment. In the same way every investment now made by us in other countries means an increase in their wealth and, consequently, in their ability to purchase our products. The war has reversed the position of America and instead of other countries increasing their sales here through increases of wealth brought about by investments in American enterprises, we are now able to increase our sales abroad upon the same principle.

World Need for Capital All the world needs capital today as a result of the war. For four years and a half the normal life of mankind has been upset. An unparalleled destruction of the things which men need for food, shelter, and clothing has taken place and the processes by which those goods are produced and placed in the hands of those who use them have been disorganized.

At the same time the nations which have been at war have been increasing their industrial capacity by the adoption of more efficient methods of production.

While Europe needs foodstuffs, raw materials, and machinery for the period during which she will be adjusting her industries to a peace basis, it is becoming increasingly evident that this industrial capacity built up during the war will be a very important factor in the rehabilitation of devastated areas.

But the fact remains that new sources of food and raw materials must be found and they can be found only through the investment of capital in those enormous areas of the earth's surface which are still undeveloped. A survey of railway construction during 1914 and of the programs then contemplated leads to the conclusion that the world then was getting ready for an era of world-wide expansion of trade and industry. It is believed now that the war will be found to have accelerated that movement.

Bases upon which America may be a Lender of Capital In view of the present world demand for capital, a survey of the bases upon which America may become a

[8]

lender of capital makes evident the opportunity which our industrial and financial leaders have of directing capital into the most profitable channels. A century and a half ago Amsterdam was the money center, partly because it was a large trading center. England, following the Napoleonic Wars, became a large lending nation because it had become a large industrial country as well as a trading center. English capital was put into French industrial enterprises, and in turn the French gradually developed an industrial capacity that gave them lending power, and Paris became a growing financial center. More recently we have seen the same development in Belgium, making Brussels a growing financial center.

Following the Franco-Prussian War, Germany started an industrial development which in time made possible the investment of German capital in other countries, and Berlin became a growing financial center.

The United States, through its whole history, with a large undeveloped area, has, generally speaking, been absorbing foreign capital as well as the growing accumulations of domestic capital. Toward the end of the nineteenth century however, it had reached such an industrial development that American capital began to seek an outlet in other countries, and there was increasing interest in world trade and the development of a merchant marine.

The United States is now in an unusually favorable situation for making foreign loans. There are available for export vast supplies of food stuffs and raw materials. According to the industrial census for 1914, the industrial plant of the United States had a total capital of $22,791,000,000, while the value of output was $24,246,000,000. The war resulted in additions to our industrial plant. This is indicated by the pig iron production,

which is about forty-five per cent. larger than before the war; the establishment of important chemicals and dyestuffs industries; and the great expansion of our shipbuilding industry. Our diversifed production and our natural resources will enable us to supply the materials which will form the material bases of loans to other countries.

As a further basis for foreign loans, this country has large absorbing power for investments. The annual savings, which amounted to $6,000,000,000 before the war, reached a total of at least $15,000,-000,000 during the war. The annual income from the balance of foreign loans, which will be due this country as a creditor nation, will probably be largely absorbed in new investments. The development of a strong and growing merchant marine will further add to our ability to invest capital in other countries. The extraordinarily large gold supply of the country, in combination with a free gold market, will give bills drawn in American dollars a world-wide reputation as synonomous with gold, and funds can be loaned payable in gold. This gold reserve is a sound basis for our credit structure—an essential requirement in an expansion program.

Nature of Foreign Investments

Credit is the keynote of business. To eliminate credit from business would hamper and restrict its opportunities. The investment of capital in domestic as well as foreign enterprises is a way of granting long term credit. There is no mystery about foreign investments. The investment of capital in other countries is really only a means of financing our export trade. The purchase of bonds of a new railroad in South America by the American investors results in all probability in the purchase in the American market of the materials and rolling stock with which that railroad is to be built and equipped. Thus, the investment of capital in other countries leads to the exportation, in the main, not of capital, but of products of American labor and capital. The proceeds of the loans will be expended for the purchase of products in this country. By financing our export trade we are, in effect, providing business for our domestic industries and in that way employment for labor.

Benefits from Foreign Investments
A loan of capital means that the lending country transfers a portion of its purchasing power to the borrowing country, and that the latter's purchasing or consuming power is increased to a corresponding extent. Loans of capital from one country to another frequently result in world-wide expansion of trade in consequence of giving such an increased purchasing power to the borrowing country. In particular such loans usually create an increased demand for the lending country's goods, and by stimulating production cause the lending country to produce a great many more goods than it otherwise would. In other words, the investment of capital increases the producing power of the lending country and increases the consuming power of the borrowing country.

The investment of capital is closely related to the problem of high prices and high cost of living. Judging from similar instances in the past, it appears that the most feasible means of reducing prices is by increasing production in proportion to population and facilitating the interchange of goods. In time, this results in an expansion of world trade, so that the volume of business may grow up to the existing supply of money and credit.

The surest way of increasing production today is to furnish the materials that European industries will need to resume operations, and to exercise our influences in establishing stabilized conditions in other countries so that the world's producing capacity may be utilized to the greatest advantage.

The investment of capital in new countries will result in an increase of production of raw materials and foodstuffs, and will create new markets for the industries of established countries.

Investment of capital in foreign countries, leading to the development of their resources, to expansion of world trade, results in a better distribution of all kinds of products to the principal markets of the world. The use of capital for the development of the tropical and sub-tropical areas has enabled people in temperate regions to obtain the products characteristic of tropical regions. The opening up of the great wheat belts of the United States and Argentina have made available a greater absolute quantity of wheat for the population of Europe and at cheaper prices. The ultimate effect of foreign investments and the expansion of world trade is to raise the standard of living by making it possible for a larger number of people to obtain those things which add to the comforts of life.

Present Need for Extension of Credit
As has been pointed out, Europe has need of foodstuffs, raw materials, and machinery to place its industrial life upon a normal basis and to give employment to its people, which is the surest way of checking the spirit of social unrest. But Europe's buying power as measured in pre-war terms is weak because she does not have that surplus of products for sale abroad which normally would be used to pay for imports. For the time being Europe must have credit extended to her in order that she may be able to buy, otherwise the period of readjustment will be prolonged and the stabilizing of her

industrial life will be delayed. Such a situation might possibly have social and political consequences which would gravely affect, not only her position, but that of other countries also. The failure to extend credit will mean that instead of our export trade expanding and growing larger, it must of necessity grow smaller until the time has come when Europe can sell us commodities in exchange for those which we send to her.

The tendency toward a decrease in our export trade was quite evident in the figures for July, which were $348,000,000 lower than those for June. The exchange situation was generally recognized as a very important factor affecting this, and it has become more unfavorable since that time. Since the Armistice the United States Government has made advances to Allied and associated Governments totalling approximately $2,250,000,000. Obviously our Government is reaching the limits of its power of making advances and it becomes imperative that the general investing public make the needed response to finance our trade, which has heretofore been done by the Government. Unless credit is extended, the buying power of Europe will become less in the immediate future and this country will be confronted with, not an expansion of exports, but a continual decrease of exports. Only an extension of long term credit can keep these markets open for our products and improve the buying power of many foreign countries.

Need for Investment of Enterprise Capital in New Countries America is interested, naturally, in the short term swing of world events, not only because of their present significance, but because of their power to influence the future in laying the bases for the development of trade and industry. From the long term viewpoint, America should play an in-

creasing part in world trade. American investors must be willing to buy foreign securities, to lend their funds for the development of other countries, particularly the development of new and undeveloped areas. This will create a growing and expanding market for American products. In addition, the return on such capital is higher because new countries have relatively high rates of interest.

But if we are to play the part of a great lending nation we must be willing, not only to lend our capital, but to lend what might rightly be termed enterprise capital; to send into these countries American men to manage industries established by American capital. These men will be able to carry American methods into the management of their enterprises. There is no greater testimony for example, to the effectiveness of the combination of capital and American management than in the copper and iron developments of Chile.

In this way the American who has funds to lend assumes the risks of an uncertain return, assumes the obligations of management, and receives larger rewards. Our young men must become imbued with the idea of going out and settling in other countries and playing their part in developing those countries and in forming an outlet for American enterprise and capital.

Liberal Credits Europe's Cardinal Need It is imperative that America today conserve her resources; that she follow a policy of the strictest economy, individual and public, in order that the absorbing power for investments may be materially increased. The necessity of financing our export trade through the extension of short and long term credit must be brought to the attention of the investing public of this country. In the first place, the appeal must be made to those people who are directly benefited by the maintenance and development of our export trade. They must be made to see that if they expect to find a market for their products, means of financing must be available. But the appeal must be made to a wider circle of individuals—the general investing public. The beneficial efforts of a period of prosperity, of a period of expansion of trade and industry, are widespread. They affect all elements of our population. It is therefore the business of every investor to do everything in his power to finance our export trade and to expand the growing foreign market for American products, through the purchase of foreign securities.

Credit is the life blood of industry. If we have faith in an individual's ability to work out his situation we are willing to give him the needed aid in the extension of credit. That is the way our domestic trade is financed. These principles are applied in ordinary business, in which the cotton planter, the manufacturer, the miner, and others obtain the means of financing their business. These principles need to be applied today to other nations and to the world at large. It is to be expected, of course, that American investors in buying foreign securities will exercise the same caution and discrimination that characterize their purchases of domestic securities. If we believe in the inherent economic strength of a country, we should be willing today to do our part toward its rehabilitation or development by extending credit. We believed in the justice of the cause of our Allies and in their ability to win finally. We extended credit to them and saw our sales to them of commodities of every kind increase beyond anything before known. In the same way extensions of credit now and in the future through foreign investments will keep those markets open for our manufacturers and traders and business will tend to grow instead of decrease with a gradual return to normal conditions. If we have faith in the future for our industry and trade, and in our economic position, we must be willing to play the constructive part, to invest capital, and to lay the bases upon which may be built a growing export trade commensurate with our position as a great nation. To do so is good business, not only for the country as a whole but also directly or indirectly, for the individual—because collective prosperity usually means individual prosperity.

Responsibility of the Borrowers   Other nations, however, must fully realize their obligations and responsibilities in seeking American capital. They must expect our people, quite naturally, to discriminate in favor of those countries with stable political conditions and governments which are imposing adequate taxation in order to meet their financial obligations on sound bases. The whole structure of our foreign investments, in fact, will rest largely upon these factors, and the extent to which we grant credit to the peoples of Europe and other countries, whether in the form of loans or investments, will be contingent almost entirely upon them.

Political stability, social order, respect for the rights of property, and a sound financial program should, of course, underlie any request for credit. That these will follow the convalescence of a world now emerging from five years of war may reasonably be expected of the nations as a whole. Duty, opportunity and work must then guide the way to service.

[12]

CPSIA information can be obtained
at www.ICGtesting.com
Printed in the USA
BVHW061657031218
534640BV00037B/3711/P

9 781334 470745